PENETRATING
THOUGHTS

31-DAY LIFE TRANSFORMING WORDS

PENETRATING
THOUGHTS

31-DAY LIFE TRANSFORMING WORDS

MICHAEL A. STRICKLAND

MEWE
Love is the more excellent way

Lithonia, GA

Scripture references are taken from the King James Version of the Holy Bible unless otherwise noted.

Pronouns for referring to the Father, Son and Holy Spirit are capitalized intentionally and the words satan and devil are never capitalized.

Publisher:
MEWE, LLC
Lithonia, GA
www.mewellc.com

Penetrating Thoughts
First Edition

ISBN: 9781732432703

Library of Congress Control Number: 2018947216

Printed in the United States of America.

In the grand scheme of life, God allows us to share the journey with individuals who leave an indelible impression in our hearts and lives forever. I am fortunate to dedicate this work to some special individuals because they have influenced my life tremendously. This intellectual property is dedicated to:

Brenda... my wife,
Briana, Morgan and Audria... my daughters,
Mrs. Linda D. Strickland... my mother, and
Rev. Dr. Hopie Strickland, Jr.... my father.

What an amazing experience my life has been. Each of these individuals' contributions has made this journey of life worthwhile. Thank you for your love, support, and confidence in my abilities.

Love ya,
Mike

FOREWORD

In his powerful 31-day Devotional, *Penetrating Thoughts*, Michael Strickland encourages us to make a conscious decision to put God first in our lives. It has often been said, "If you're too busy for God, you're too busy," and, "You always have time for the things you put first."

If you find your days spinning out of control, it's time to do a self-evaluation of your routine. Are your prayers only being said if you happen to remember before a meal, or do you find yourself saying a quick one-minute prayer before bed out of guilt because you haven't talked to Him at all during the day? If so, I challenge you to commit yourself to a month of reading Pastor Strickland's easy, yet life-changing principles.

This booklet will guide you into an intimate relationship with the Creator of the Universe. This incredible devotional will allow you to launch out into a deep relationship with God that your soul cries out for, and leave behind the shallow waters that the enemy of our souls tries so desperately to hold us in.

Dr. Chris Bowen, CEO/Founder
5 Star Personal and Corporate Development

INTRODUCTION

Penetrate ~ to enter the interior of; to enter and diffuse itself
through; to affect or deeply impress the mind of feelings

Diikneomai Gr. ~ to go through, penetrate; pierce

As a visual learner, my thoughts will be accompanied by illustrations that speak to your mind. Please allow the Spirit of God to speak to you as you meditate on your thoughts, and as you visualize their significance in your mind. Imagine how much more effective it would be if your thoughts pierced the very fabric of your life, thereby causing you to experience God in an unprecedented way.

Elisha A. Hoffman penned these words:

What a fellowship, what a joy divine…
Leaning on the EVERLASTING Arms.
Oh how sweet to walk in this pilgrim way…
Oh how bright the path grows from day to day…
What have I to dread, what have I to fear…
I have blessed peace with my Lord so near…

The underlying message of these words is, "The ancient God is a firm foundation eternally." How awesome it is to know that the arms of our God are strong enough for us to lean, wide enough to embrace us, and tough enough to keep us from falling!

As a preacher's kid a.k.a. a PK, the trajectory of my life changed when I discovered the importance of having a healthy vertical relationship with God, which in turn, adjusted my horizontal relationship with other people. The "Who-ness" of God is the LOVE of God. The "Where-ness" of God is omnipresent. The "How-ness" of God is making miraculous ways. This perspective helps us release true love and impart it onto others.

To that end, I have also come to realize that if I make quality, quiet, and uninterrupted time with God, my plans will come to fruition. Proverbs 16:3 speaks to us accordingly: *"Commit thy works unto the Lord, and thy thoughts shall be established."* That word "commit" suggests that I must make the choice to dedicate a portion of my daily life to spending time with God. As I plan and walk in His purpose, I "commit" myself to God and "put" Him in charge of the work that I am doing.

Putting God in charge of your life is a conscious decision – a decision that, if done consistently, will transform your life. This is a moment of penetration; God is in you, and you are in Him. This is a moment where intimacy, or "in-to-me, God you see," grows. This is not just a passing segment of time, but a real space that encompasses the breadth and depth of supernatural transfers and exchanges. Amid all the adjustments and challenges that we face daily, we must desire God more, hunger for His presence deeply, and yearn for Him continually.

I encourage you to commit yourself to being transformed by the renewing of your mind. Surrender your "you" to God and receive God's "you" in order to get what God intends out of "you."

I invite you to join me as I share thoughts with you that will pierce your thinking and cause you to meditate on the same revelations that have transformed my life…Let's journey together!

Michael A. Strickland

MY ROOTS NEED A ROTOR

Today's Penetrating Thought: Don't let your roots determine your routes if your roots are rotten.

But Blessed is the man who trusts me, God, the woman who sticks with God, They're like trees replanted in Eden, putting down roots near the rivers – Never a worry through the hottest of summers, never dropping a leaf, Serene and calm through droughts, bearing fresh fruit in every season (Jeremiah 17:7-8, MSG).

PENETRATING MOMENT: What motivations drive your words, thoughts, and desires? I want to challenge you today to take a good look at yourself and to stop blaming the enemy. Sometimes the roots that anchor us are rendered toxic from bitter experiences, and we need to make them healthy with the antidote of the next season in our lives.

There are certain things in our lives that we need to reevaluate because the substratum of our thoughts is a place where that which is rotten resides. Our root system needs to be purified before it can bear fruit again. Ask yourself: what have I allowed to take hold of the goodness in my life and infect it? Who is mixed in my roots? What has been hidden away in my subconscious for so long that I refuse to soften it, heal it and extricate it once and for all?

Job 29:19 ~ My roots are deep!
Psalm 1:3 ~ I am planted and revitalized by the water!
Psalm 92:12 ~ I am the righteous and I flourish!
Isaiah 61:3 ~ The splendor of the Lord is displayed!
Jeremiah 17:8 ~ I'm blessed in every condition!

PRAYER

Father, today as we desire to live holy lives acceptable unto You, please strengthen us to confront what needs to be conquered. We pray that You will.

Break: *We interrupt the regularly scheduled program to bring you this breaking news story... I will make sure that my roots are neither cluttered nor crowded! If I have allowed the dirt to harden, Father, forgive me and wash me clean in the Blood of Jesus!*

THE ANT MENTALITY

You lazy fool, look at an ant. Watch it closely; let it teach you a thing or two. Nobody has to tell it what to do. All summer it stores up food; at harvest it stockpiles provisions. So how long are you going to laze around doing nothing? How long before you get out of bed? A nap here, a nap there, a day off here, a day off there, sit back, take it easy – do you know what comes next? Just this: you can look forward to a dirt-poor life, poverty your permanent houseguest (Proverbs 6:6, MSG)!

PENETRATING MOMENT: Most of us have seen ants building mounds of dirt wherever they can. They're making sure that their stockpiles can be easily retrieved, no matter what the weather's like. Sometimes, when a person sees an ant pile, they want to sweep it away because of its unattractive appearance. Note that even if the ant pile is swept away, the ant's resolve is not broken; it carries on even after witnessing that which took it time and energy to build being reduced to nothingness.

Nothing stops an ant from completing its tasks. Ants will tirelessly build until they have stockpiled enough resources for the next season. The ant's mentality is to make it happen… no matter what circumstances befall it!

Today, I want you to get up and stop making excuses in this season of your life. Seek the guidance that you know you need to move past and beyond your circumstances. Stand up in the power of the Lord, the one who is in control of your life, and make it happen. You are indeed well able to do this. Whatever your "this" is, you can indeed do it and you will recover.

You do not need anyone's permission to make what God has promised for you in your life come to pass. Invest in yourself; look at those who oppose you, and use their opposition as a stepping stone to MOVE upwards and onwards. The ant teaches us that we cannot place our responsibilities in the hands of other people and anticipate that they will be fulfilled. God has invested in you, so that YOU can invest in yourself!

PRAYER

Father, today as we learn the lesson from the ant, we pray that You will fortify us with endurance to see it through in this season of our lives. We thank You for using the ant to teach us that perseverance yields completion and provision.

Break: *We interrupt the regularly scheduled program to bring you this breaking news story...I can do all things through Christ who strengthens me!*

MY TRANSITION IS TRANSFORMATIVE

Romans 12:2b … after the "but" …

~⟲~

PENETRATING MOMENT: My mind is transformed to accommodate a transition. There are some vital pieces of advice that I wish to infuse your mind with today:

1. Always stay focused on what is in front of you.

2. Make your worship of and devotion to God central to your life.

3. Keep your root system intact, healthy, and watered.

Just because something changes doesn't mean it has transformed. Sometimes change can be rejected, but if a true transformation has taken place in your life, you will migrate from change to transformation regardless.

Those who have experienced a transformation will adjust to their environment and align their perspectives with the Word of God, when the time is right. Since

God has blessed you to live with purpose, I encourage you to take a moment to consider the following questions:

1. How will you move from change to transformation, so that you may effectively and positively affect what you see?

2. What areas of your life need to be adjusted before a complete transformation can take place?

3. Who, if anyone, needs to be in your presence to facilitate your transformation?

Don't just change for the present with yesterday's mentality. A 'yesterday mentality' will inevitably take you back to yesterday, so instead, transform for the future and the newness it brings.

PRAYER

Abba Father, it is to You that we give all glory, honor, praise, adoration and thanksgiving. Today, as we embrace the process of transformation, we pray that our minds can comprehend what You intend for our lives. Help us remain in You.

Break: *We interrupt the regularly scheduled program to bring you this breaking news story... I am changing for the better, and I like it!*

MY TRAJECTORY HAS CHANGED

Come and follow Me, and I'll send you to catch people
instead of fish (Mark 1:17, TV).

In this passage, you will find that Jesus is interrupting the ordinary flow of the lives of the men He chose. These men were doing what they did best, which seemed to be working well for them in their own lives.

Their profession involved catching fish; an activity which they had clearly perfected. Jesus suddenly comes along and interrupts their regularly scheduled routines. What do you do when it is Jesus who makes the interruption and changes the trajectory of your ENTIRE life?

—⊙—

PENETRATING MOMENT: Settling into and sticking to a daily routine is something which we can all relate to. For someone like myself, I can become accustomed to a certain way of life, and that can become the prescribed manner in which my life's events unfold.

It was not until I met Jesus that I discovered that life can and needs to be altered from time to time for me to truly experience the more and the greater that I feel inside of me.

Allow me to encourage you today to lay claim to the fact that, for God to get out of us what He intends to use, we have to make specific detours in our lives. Jesus hand picks and singles out the individuals whom He wants for His purposes, and it is His responsibility to make us into who He wants us to become.

Don't fight the path to change; trust in the Path Changer and watch what He transforms you into.

PRAYER

Father, we thank You that You have chosen us to follow You. We trust You to make us into the disciples that You want us to be. It is ours to follow and it is Yours to make. Thank You that You decided what my results will be as I agree with the path changes in my life. I delight in Your will and lean not on my own understanding, but in all of my ways I will acknowledge You, as You direct my path.

Break: *We interrupt the regularly scheduled program to bring you this breaking news story…I'm headed in a new direction… one which I've not traveled before!*

I Re-"present" Who I Represent

Now that I've put you there on a hilltop, on a light stand—shine! Keep open house; be generous with your lives. By opening up to others, you'll prompt people to open up with God, this generous Father in heaven (Matthew 5:16, MSG).

PENETRATING MOMENT: Matthew admonishes us to make sure that the one who others see and the one who has already been seen by Him are one in the same. The temptation to show off who are, or who we think we are, while disallowing God to shine in and through us, is understandably great.

Today, I encourage you to live the meaning of the prefix, "re." It simply means to do over; to repeat. Imitate Christ and His righteousness.

Reproduce what you see in Him. He is to be re-presented, and we are to represent what He stands for. This is because your life is not your own; it has been paid for with a price... in fact, it has been paid for with the ultimate price.

Therefore, glorify God in your body, in your mind, and in your spirit, all of which belong to the Lord.

> ## PRAYER
>
> *Father help me today to not go out and shine my own light, but to let the light of Christ shine through me so that others will see the works that You've assigned and give You the credit. Help me to fully re-present who I represent: Christ. As Christ commissioned in the new commandment, I should love others and, by this, all men will know who I belong to.*

Break: *We interrupt the regularly scheduled program to bring you this breaking news story... Re-present who you represent. My life is not my own... it belongs to God, for Him to use for His purpose, honor and glory.*

I'll Do It Again If You Say So

Master, we've been fishing all night, and we haven't caught even a minnow. But . . . all right, I'll do it if You say so (Luke 5:5, MSG).

Amid my confusion, Jesus says, "Do it again ..."
Amid my ignorance of the outcome, Jesus says, "Do it again ..."
Amid my emotions of despair and hopelessness, Jesus says, "Do it again ..."
While recognizing your fruitless efforts, Jesus still says, "Do it again ..."

Penetrating Moment: Sometimes, we are reluctant to engage in "do-overs." The amount of time and energy spent on an endeavor is critical and if once a certain amount of time has passed, we do not see any results, we may feel that God is trying to tell us something about our efforts.

What I have learned, however, is that God will instruct us to let down the nets one more time. Since He already knows what He's going to do, He instructs us to go at it again. Allow me to encourage you today to walk with me as we let down our nets to:

- Forgive, one more time...

- Embrace, one more time...
- Talk about it, one more time...
- Shine the light, one more time...
- Rebuild it, one more time...
- Adjust it, one more time...
- Return, one more time...

This may be the appointed time for God Himself to increase and show Himself to be mighty in the very situation that you have washed your hands clean of. Today is the day to do it...**One More Time!**

> ## PRAYER
> *Father, give us strength to do it just one more time. We will obey Your word and we will cast our nets out and do it again, just because You said it. We trust that You know the desired outcome of the "nevertheless" You have instructed us to walk in. And so, strengthen us today so that we can do it at Your word.*

Break: *We interrupt the regularly scheduled program to bring you this breaking news story...I am doing it again, even though I have failed. Nevertheless, I will do it again because the Lord said so!* Today, we say "Yes" to the "again."

THE BLUE SCREEN

What do you do when things are about to crash?

We know that every time we boot a computer, we expect to see a screen that displays software programs for our use. We regularly click on various icons that are pathways to the software programs that we want. It becomes a habit of ours to hit the power button, log in and click away, but what happens when your computer is about to reach the end of its life? A warning screen pops up with a lot of letters and numbers that don't make sense to many of us, but one thing we do understand is that something bad is about to happen to the computer.

What happens in the crash?

- Items/things are lost
- Files are erased
- Systems need to be replaced
- Software is wiped out
- Viruses infect the computer
- Hard drive needs attention

PENETRATING MOMENT: In Exodus 14, things were about to "crash" for the children of Israel because of what was in front of them and who was behind them. In today's terms, I would liken that to a computer that's about to crash. We should always remember, however, that no matter what the problem, God always has a plan in place when it appears that things are about to reach their end for us. In the Scripture, it was God's plan to teach the children that He is worthy to be trusted. When we can't see a way out, He will make a way!

I want this truth to penetrate your mind today because there are certain situations in our lives that will cause us to think that we are about to see a blue screen. But take heart today and KNOW that God has a protection plan from the blue screens of your life. Now unto Him who is able to keep you from falling …

PRAYER

Father, thank You for protecting us in the midst of what seems to be about to crash. We lean and depend on You because You are our Sustainable Substratum upon which we build our lives. We declare and decree that our world will not crash and it will not turn blue on us. You did it before, and we believe that You will do it again.

Break: *We interrupt the regularly scheduled program to bring you this breaking news story... God is making a Way through for us!*

I'M READY TO BE

In Luke 19, the ten servants who were called together were given the commission to occupy until the return of the owner who was being appointed king.

This Scripture teaches us that the intent was for the servants to fill the owner's position until he returned. This suggests that the post was to "be" occupied until the return of the owner.

"Be" is the ability to act in the now, in the moment. In the sense of the present, it means "to fill now."

PENETRATING MOMENT: I challenge you today to go out and **"Be:"**

A ~ Awesome   F ~ Forgiving
B ~ Brave   G ~ Giving
C ~ Courageous   H ~ Honest
D ~ Defeat-less   I ~ Integrated
E ~ Effective   J ~ Justified

K ~ Kind
L ~ Loving
M ~ Motivating
N ~ Nurturing
O ~ Optimistic
P ~ Patient
Q ~ Quintessential
R ~ Righteous

S ~ Successful
T ~ Tenacious
U ~ Unwavering
V ~ Vivified
W ~ Working
X ~ Xtra-ordinary
Y ~ Yielding
Z ~ Zealous

PRAYER

Father, in the vicissitudes of life and situations we find ourselves in, please help us to "be" in the present moment that we are in. Give us the grace to relish and enjoy opportunities moment by moment.

Break: *We interrupt the regularly scheduled program to bring you this breaking news story… I will "be" in the moment that God has afforded me in the present!*

CHAPTER 42 IS COMING

In the Bible, Job is depicted as a man who knew how to wait on the Lord. In the children's choir in the 70's, we used to sing a song that included these words: "If Job waited on the Lord, then why can't I, Oh Why can't I?" It went on to say, "Job waited 'til the flesh fell from his bones, all the hope that Job had was gone."

The trials and tribulations of Job are often recalled whenever we speak about waiting on God and living through periods of having, losing, and WAITING to recover.

Job: the upright man, the blameless man, the one who feared God and shunned evil, had to endure the process before he could enjoy the progress.

———⊙———

PENETRATING MOMENT: Today, I want to encourage you to KNOW that Chapter 42 in your life is coming. Job endured his trials and tribulations, BUT, when you read the last chapter of the Book of Job (Chapter 42), you will see why the rewards were worth the wait. When it comes to waiting, Romans 8 teaches us that... *We are enlarged in the waiting. We, of course, don't see what is enlarging us. But the longer we wait, the larger we become, and the more joyful our expectancy.*

Today I say: wait. Wait, because you are not as ready as you think you are. Wait, because God knows how long this season needs to last in your life. Wait, I say, because the "due" season will not bear fruit otherwise. Wait, I say, for God is perfecting you; He's pruning you; He's preparing you; He's maturing you; He's molding you; He's emptying you; He's filling you; He's reshaping/shaping you to be what HE wants you to be.

James Cleveland penned these words: "Please be patient with me; God is not through with me... Oh but when God gets through with me, I shall come forth as PURE gold." After 41 Chapters in the Book of Job, we discover that the Lord greatly blessed the latter part of his life with joy and abundance.

PRAYER

Father, today we just trust the process. Thank You that You have not removed Yourself from us, but You are closer than close. We adore the fact that You are the Processor and we are the processed, so we rely on You.

Break: *We interrupt the regularly scheduled program to bring you this breaking news story... I will wait on you, Lord, for I trust your process!*

Everybody Is Not with You

In Judges 7, we see an example where some cutting away was necessary to achieve victory. God instructs Gideon to release most of the fighting men with these words:

> *And the Lord said unto Gideon, The people that are with thee*
> *are too many for me to give the Midianites into their hands,*
> *lest Israel vaunt themselves against me, saying, Mine own*
> *hand hath saved me* (Judges 7:2, KJV).

There are some connections in your life that need to be severed before victory can be achieved throughout it. Thank God for those who helped you reach your current stage, BUT, for the next season, know that they cannot help you survive or thrive.

Let me be clear: they are still good people; it's just that for what is about to happen to you and through you in your life, they are neither equipped to take you to the next season nor go there with you.

Learn to embrace the toughness of "cutting" away. God instructed Gideon in this fashion because He knew the heart of the people of Israel, in that if they had more than the enemy, they could simply say, "We did this!" God alone knows the ones who will help you achieve victory, yet still give Him the Glory.

The people will see your good work and glorify God!

—◎—

PENETRATING MOMENT: Take advantage of today. Let God purge you as only He can. Allow Him to drain the pond of less to make room for a lake of more. He knows what, who and how many are necessary to remain in your life so that His agenda for your life WILL be accomplished.

PRAYER

Father, we thank You for being in total control of our lives. We embrace the movement that is taking place in our lives as the seasons change. We declare that You are indeed the source of all and are a part of all. Help us to remain relational as we trust the shifts You are making in our lives.

Break: *We interrupt the regularly scheduled program to bring you this breaking news story... I will trust God to add and subtract in my life as He sees fit!*

DO YOU SEE WHAT I SEE?

The late Dr. Myles Monroe once said:

> *Vision is the key to <u>unlocking the gates</u> (entry way; the portal that lets me into) of what was (my now) and what is (my what's to come), to <u>propelling</u> (spur, drive, gush) us into the land of what could be (my next), and has not yet been.*

Habakkuk 2:2, MSG ~ *"Write what you see. Write it out in BIG BLOCK LETTERS so that it can be read on the run."*

God says: "Write what you see."

It has to be that, no matter what circumstance you find yourself in, the vision keeps you moving. This vision-message is a witness pointing to what's ahead. It speaks to what will manifest. Why?

The block letters are recommended so you can see them even when you don't feel it. The BLOCK LETTERS will steer the ship, even when the passengers don't want to go.

So, as we move ahead with the revelation, it needs to be large enough for us to see so that we keep moving in the direction of what is revealed.

———⊙———

PENETRATING MOMENT: Today, I will:

- Raise my expectation (strong belief that something will happen),
- Release my FAITH,
- See what I saw, and
- Lay aside every weight and the sin that hinders me, and look up and keep moving!

My vision sets me in a posture of PRESS and I will let NO-thing hinder what God has revealed. God's plan is to prosper me; God did not give me the spirit of FEAR; I will get to the place where EYES HAVE NOT SEEN, NOR EARS HEARD!!

PRAYER

Father, I thank You for the revelatory vision that You showed me. I pray for strength and wisdom as I continue to see what I saw when You said what You said. I tune my ear to the rhythm of heaven, as the vision message speaks to what shall be.

Break: *We interrupt the regularly scheduled program to bring you this breaking news story ... What I saw will happen in my life, in Jesus' Name.*

BUILD ON WHAT?

It won't fall if the WORD is SOLID …

These words I speak to you are not incidental additions to your life, homeowner improvements to your standard of living. They are foundational words, words to build a life on. If you work these words into your life, you are like a smart carpenter who built his house on solid rock. Rain poured down, the river flooded, a tornado hit—but nothing moved that house. It was fixed to the rock (Matthew 7:24-27, MSG).

In this passage, Jesus teaches us that our lives should be built on the foundation of His word to provide an anchor for our daily lives. WOW!! We are all faced with things that hit us at moments we think we are prepared for. But when they hit, we realize we were not as prepared as we thought (in our day, we called them "sucker punch moments").

What do you do when life hits you in a place, in a space and in a location where your very foundation is shaken? How do you respond when the tough stuff that you didn't plan for and the rough stuff that you didn't see hit you below the belt? It's those things that hit you even when your guard is up – they throw a punch on your blind side.

I'm not saying to you that bad things won't happen. I'm saying that, as they do and when they do, your substratum (base/core) has to have as its hooking place – The WORD of GOD.

–◎–

PENETRATING MOMENT: I ask that today you be not just a speaking hearer, but an obedient doer of the WORD of God. The WORD holds you together; the WORD builds your stamina; the WORD guides your way; the WORD keeps the joints and marrow in place in your life. SO LET'S BUILD ON THE WORD!!

In the children's book, *The Three Little Pigs*, the wolf comes and applies pressure to the house that the three pigs built. If you are familiar with the fable, the pigs built their houses out of straw, wood and bricks. When the attack came, the type of materials was crucial. What material are you using to build your house?

> # PRAYER
>
> *Father, we thank You that Your word is a lamp and a light. Today, we stand in faith knowing that man does not live by bread alone but by every word that proceeds out of Your mouth. We want to make Your word more than just ink on a page, but oil in our lives.*

Break: *We interrupt the regularly scheduled program to bring you this breaking news story ... I am built on a solid rock and a firm foundation – The WORD of God!!*

THANK GOD I'M NOT IN THERE!

Transparent Moment: I was driving to work today and this mortuary that I pass almost twice a week stood out. I see it regularly, but it zoomed into view this day. I immediately began to thank God that, of all the places I could be, I was glad I was not in there.

I am not sure what the Spirit was saying to me, but I felt in my spirit an overwhelming joy that I am still alive and have the use of my limbs and all my faculties. I went into thanksgiving mode because, regardless of all the things I could complain about, I live.

Penetrating Moment: 2 Kings 20:6 ~ God speaks to Hezekiah and says, "I will add fifteen years to your life." You will not die before the finished work that God Himself has prepared and planned for you.

You need to stop killing a thing that God intended to live. Live every moment as a moment of victory. Never stop at a comma because God has more. Stop putting a period where God has not put one.

There is more to your story and your life. Refocus, and let the fact that you made it penetrate your mind to know that, for the rest of your days, you should give God the praise.

PRAYER

God, I thank You today that, because You let me see this day, I still have more to do for You and the Kingdom. I ask that You forgive me for calling it quits, when You are only turning the page in my life. Help me to see it the way You see it and call it what You will. I pray that this day I live my life to its maximum because You are walking with me. I declare today that it is not done until You say it's done.

Break: *We interrupt the regularly scheduled program to bring you this breaking news story ... My life is filled with life!! LIVE with PURPOSE!*

I'M TREMBLING BUT I'M TRUSTING

But when he remembered how strong the wind was, his courage
caught in his throat and he began to sink (Matthew 14:30, TV).

—⊙—

PENETRATING MOMENT: I must give Peter credit for the move. It was, you can imagine, a tough decision to step into a place where nothing visible would support Peter's getting out of the boat. It was brave of him to leave the level of comfort that he grew to know. It was a powerful testimony that he would venture OUT into a new norm.

Peter's courage to move his feet from solid to unstable speaks volumes. Anytime there is a shift and an adjustment, it requires a great deal of courage. Peter in this episode demonstrates what trembling and trust look like. As Peter ventured out, he trembled.

I want to address your fear today and let it know that it is False Evidence Appearing Real in your life. Fear is a handicapper and will choke out the move of God – that is, if you give in to it. In spite of the others who may want you to remain in the boat because they are scared, I challenge you today to hear the voice of God, and move out regardless of the tremble you feel.

Peter kept his eyes on the One who called, and walked in a place where apparently nothing supported him. It was only when he took his eyes off of the One who called that he began to sink.

PRAYER

Today, Father, I pray that it is at Your word that we move. We release the chains of fear, doubt and unbelief off our lives so that we may trust You in all things. We confess that You are always with us and that You uphold us with Your righteous right hand. We declare freedom from "fear"dom, in Jesus' Name.

Break: *We interrupt the regularly scheduled program to bring you this breaking news story... I will trust in the midst of the tremble because I know Who is with me!!*

TURNING POINT TRANSITION SEASON

Okay, I am about to reveal my age now. Do you remember when we had to turn the knob on the car radio to find the right station? In the Cadillac, the panel had station numbers where you could set the little red line to tune into the station of your choice.

There were also little lines in between the numbers that allowed you to fine-tune your station. The interesting thing about the panel was that, if you didn't turn the knob just right, you would get static and sometimes the static would drown out the news from the station you had selected (the frequency).

PENETRATING MOMENT: In life, we like to get into a mode where we can predict what the sound of our position will be. We enjoy having the control knob in our hands. But what I have come to discover is that, as seasons of our lives are adjusted, we can miss the mark and not press through the static that often happens in the midst of change.

We can miss the next season because we didn't push through the static enough.

Ecclesiastes 3:2-3 teaches us that there are specific seasons, but then there are also static seasons. The static seasons are the ones where the *"and"* comes between the seasons.

> *A right time to plant and another to reap,*
> *A right time to kill and another to heal,*
> *A right time to destroy and another to construct ...(MSG)*

The *"and"* suggests that there is an experience of one thing but, in order to successfully make it to the next state, a change must take place. If you want to pluck, you must sow first. Joy comes after the pain.

I encourage you to make it through the "and's." If you can make it through the "and's," in your life, you can enjoy the rewards of "after the and's."

PRAYER

God, help me in the in-between stations/seasons of life where I don't quite understand what is taking place. But, by faith, I KNOW that, in the end, You make everything beautiful in itself and in its time.

Break: *We interrupt the regularly scheduled program to bring you this breaking news story ... I am Going to Turn the Corner successfully and I will not quit!!*

I DON'T HAVE TIME FOR THIS

"I have to get this done…"

"I've got to meet this person…"

"I must close this deal…"

"I have to set one more thing in place before I finalize this plan…"

"I have to make sure my 'to do' list has all the necessary check marks beside it so that I can feel a sense of accomplishment today…"

I can hear all of the voices that speak to you in your mind reminding you of all the THINGS that you have to get done "yesterday." We are told that champions survive by the "list" that they create for themselves. But before this topic penetrates your mind, I need for you to inhale and exhale. Of all the things in life that can be relived or regained, time is not one of them. Time is what God provides for us as He allows us to live what HE has purposed for us.

———⊙———

PENETRATING MOMENT: The moment that you are living in is now and it is the only moment that you really have. We can wish and dream of having more of that moment, but the truth of the matter is all we have is "this" moment. I hear you saying:

- If I had more hours in the day, I would _____.
- Life demands too much.
- I'm tired because _____.
- Too many people are depending on me to get it done.

Get into a rhythm so that you can prioritize your daily schedule as you devote your early thoughts and plans to God.

It is said that "Money moves in the morning." Well, before the money moves, spend time with God so that He can help you spend His money in a manner that pleases Him.

PRAYER

Father, please don't let me get too busy and tied down with the necessities of life that I purposely have to "make" time to spend with You. Help me rearrange and prioritize my agenda so that "You" are glorified.

Break: *We interrupt the regularly scheduled program to bring you this breaking news story ... I am Available for and to YOU!!!*

THE PAIN WAS FOR THE REIGN

If we stick it out with him, we'll rule with him (1 Peter 2:12, MSG).

Today, I can hear it in you ... "If this transition season presents me with another segment of my life that needs to be developed, I'm going to shut it down and quit the race. If I have to be cut one more time to produce more character in me, then keep the knife and the scalpel because I have don't have any more shaving room! If I must endure one more hardship as a good solider! If I have one more trial that I have to triumph over..."

PENETRATING MOMENT: Paul says that staying the course will cause you to rule and reign with Christ. In a transition season, be encouraged to know that the birth is going to happen. It is during the birthing season that you must remain tough.

Some stages in these seasons will include:

- Revelation
- Conception

- Nutrition
- Incubation
- Nurturing

And, as in the after-birth, there is the placenta – the part that the baby once fed on but can't be used after birth. Revelation: there are some people who grew up with you and ate what they needed, but when the baby is born, they can't eat what is takes to make the baby mature. Know who needs to be with you in what season. Recognize who is weighty. Identify who needs to be cut like the umbilical cord. Know who is anointed for the ahead journey.

> ## PRAYER
>
> *Father, we repent of having doubted this season in our lives. We ask now that You open our eyes to know who needs to be a part of this birthing season we are in right now. We pray for strength to endure the journey so as to persevere through all the stages of the process.*

Break: *We interrupt the regularly scheduled program to bring you this breaking news story... I am like a tree planted by the waters. I shall NOT be MOVED!!*

EVERYTHING IS ALL-READY ALL-RIGHT

Today we begin our day with a Newsflash!!! Romans 8:28 is still in the Bible and it reads: *That's why we can be so sure that every detail in our lives of love for God is worked into something good* (MSG).

In situations where we must learn to wait in the process, we can become concerned that some things are not going the way we expect. We begin to think that God is not with us or that His plan for our lives has changed. We may harbor a sense of being abandoned.

~──⊙──~

PENETRATING MOMENT: The weary moments in our lives happen when we are in the period of waiting on what God has spoken till they manifest. Those moments should be undergirded by the knowledge that the Spirit communicates with God on our behalf at times when we don't have the words to describe how we feel; indeed, don't know how we should pray.

Be encouraged to know that your tears are interpreted; your moans and groans are interpreted; your sighs of helplessness are interpreted; the moving of your mouth and no-thing heard is interpreted … God's Spirit is right alongside us, helping us along. HE knows us far better than we know ourselves, and brings our cries before God.

Anytime my current situations are "brought" before God, I can shout in the fact that Everything is ALL-ready ALL-right.

PRAYER

Father, I pray that, as I live my life, I recognize that everything is already alright. There is no-thing that is going to be, but everything is already alright.

Break: *We interrupt the regularly scheduled program to bring you this breaking news story … "Every"thing is "ALL"ready "ALL" right!!!*

GO BACK AND DO IT RIGHT

*And he went on his journeys from the south even to Bethel, unto
the place where his tent had been at the beginning, between
Bethel and Ai; Unto the place of the altar, which he had made
there at the first: and there Abram called on the name of the
LORD (Genesis 13:3-4, KJV).*

I will be very open and honest today. As a leader who has made several mistakes in life, I went through a period where I felt no one was with me and I was blackballed in the community where I serve as Lead Pastor. In the midst of that aloneness, I began to replay moments and times in which I felt the people that had left had done so because of something that I had said or done or something they had heard about me. The torture of being haunted by that suspicion, aggravated by having to face the congregation, was often too tough to bear. I felt some people had wronged me, and I had allowed a grudge to develop.

Some days later at a conference, the Lord began to deal with me on the subject of forgiveness. The Word of the Lord spoke to me very firmly. It had me send messages to the individuals who I needed to clear the air with so that my Father in Heaven could bless me. Matthew 6:14-15 says, *"In prayer there is a connection between what God does and what you do. You can't get forgiveness from God, for instance, without also forgiving others. If you refuse to do your part, you cut yourself off from God's part"* (MSG).

PENETRATING MOMENT: Listen to the voice of God and obey His command to go back to the people, places and events that you feel have held you captive. The forgiveness that you seek is not just for the other person. It is primarily for you to free yourself from the bondage and pain that are attached to the episodes in your life that you keep reliving internally. God made Abram retrace his steps back to the place where he messed up to mend the breach. Sometimes, the people who hurt you go unscathed, but you know in your heart that you need to forgive them because of a broken covenant!!

PRAYER

Father, as You have forgiven me, I pray that I can bring myself to the place where I can recognize that I have shown only surface forgiveness. But deep down, I know that I need to forgive and seek the forgiveness of others so that I can be freed from these thoughts and feelings that keep coming back. Help me lift the weight to free my life, in Jesus' most forgiving and powerful name, Amen.

Break: *We interrupt the regularly scheduled program to bring you this breaking news story ... I will seek the forgiveness that I need in order to be set free!!*

I AM "THAT," YES, I AM

And God said unto Moses, I AM THAT I AM: and he said, Thus shalt thou say unto the children of Israel, I AM hath sent me unto you (Exodus 3:14, KJV).

PENETRATING MOMENT: We often go through trials where we need someone to be there for us. We find ourselves in predicaments which we feel could be solved if only someone understood, felt, recognized, or even cared for us.

We feel a cry for someone to empathize with the "that" which we feel. In Exodus 3, God speaks to Moses and instructs him to tell the people that He is the "that" – *"I AM THAT I AM."* If we apply the text, God is saying to us:

- In healing, I am that – The Healer.
- In providing, I am that – The Provider.
- In mending, I am that – The Mender.
- In sickness, I am that – The Deliverer.
- In a fight, I am that – The Fighter.

In essence, no matter what you fill in the blank with, God says, I am the "that" and I Am all the "that" that you need. We trust in the Great I AM.

PRAYER

Father, forgive us for the times we felt You were not strong and capable enough to handle the creatures You created. With all of Your strength and power, You are indeed ABLE to be all the "that" that we will ever need. Today, we stand in agreement with the truth that You spoke to Moses in Exodus: You are the Great I Am...

Break: *We interrupt the regularly scheduled program to bring you this breaking news story ... I know that the Great I am is just that... I AM!!*

FORGIVE TO HEAL

*Confess your faults one to another, and pray one for another, that ye may be healed. The effectual fervent prayer of a righteous man availeth much (*James 5:16, KJV).

Many of our sicknesses and inner issues are brought upon us by our tendency to hold on to things, events, encounters, people, failures, mess-ups.

PENETRATING MOMENT: There are times and moments in all of our lives where we have to admit, "I'm NOT proud of this."

- It could be a decision we've made;
- It could be a choice we've made;
- It could be a connection/disconnection that we made; or
- It could be a missed-move that we made;
- It could have been an unwelcome violation of our property without our permission.

We often progress through the vicissitudes of life learning to cope with things the "best way we can." We develop tools and strategies that support our determination to hold on and never forgive so that we might be healed.

I've come to learn that there is a reason that people live with the tension and struggle of the replaying of their mishaps. It is because we do NOT have a safe haven to run to, to confess and trust that the healing will take place. Not only healing, but the assurance that confidentiality will be met. So, we learn to mask an inward struggle caused by the absence of making the necessary confession in prayer with another, which leads to healing. Today, I encourage you to take the opportunity to discover a haven where you can release your hurts, and be healed.

PRAYER

Father, I pray for the person reading this penetrating thought today that You will give them the strength, energy, timing and the wisdom of HOW TO FORGIVE to HEAL. It hurts, God; it weighs heavy, God; it impedes their progress, God; it keeps flashing by like a stalker, God; it feels like it will never end, God. And so today, I stand as an intercessor who had to find a haven himself in order to forgive. I declare and decree that it is possible and is do-able, in Jesus' Name. Pause here and let the Lord minister to you as this process is not as simple as a change of clothes. This is a decision to make a life change to remove the guilt, shame and pain that accompanies the confession to another.

Break: *We interrupt the regularly scheduled program of UNFORGIVENESS to bring you this breaking news story...Today I FORGIVE because I want to be HEALED for real!!*

SHOUT IT DOWN

So the people shouted, and priests blew the trumpets; and when the people heard the sound of the trumpet, the people shouted with a great shout and the wall fell down flat, so that the people went up into the city, every man straight ahead, and they took the city (Joshua 6:20, KJV).

Today, I want to speak to your shout. It is recorded that impenetrable walls came down with a shout. Not a holler, but a SHOUT. Joshua had instructed the Israelites that, when they heard the sound of the shofar, they were to shout. WOW! The Hebrew word for shout – "Shabach" – means to address in a loud voice; to commend. Well, when you shout, you are addressing God in a loud voice that extols something He has done.

PENETRATING MOMENT: Most individuals underestimate the power in a "shout." Your atmosphere shifts when you release a sound that breaks the surrounding wave patterns. Ever felt pained to the core? Turmoil until you could not stand it? Tough situations that gripped you tighter than a vice? Years of grief and despair? Well, today, I am here to tell you that, if you can see those situations as something behind you, then I urge you to shout. God is so AMAZING and so AWESOME because He is always doing something that makes me wanna shout.

No matter what life is throwing at you right now, I want you to do this with me … Throw your head back. Lift up your hands. Get into position and shout! Shout because the Lord has done marvelous things in your life. The Lord has set ambushes upon the enemy. The Lord has released the city into your hands… SHOUT!!!!!!!!

PRAYER

*Father, in the name of Jesus. I declare and I decree that my mouth will not remain closed. I have been silent long enough. I will release a shout into the atmosphere, causing walls that for years have blocked, hindered, stopped and delayed my breakthrough to come down. I WILL FOREVER OPEN MY MOUTH AND **GIVE** YOU PRAISE!! Forgive me for making You wait for me to open my mouth. I now offer a shout unto YOU. Simply because You are worthy, will I do it, simply because you are the Great I AM. I will do it because I remember it was You God who first did it for me.*

Break: *We interrupt the regularly scheduled program of UNFORGIVENESS to bring you this breaking news story… I will open up my mouth and SHOUT the walls down.*

IT MUST OBEY...

Jesus says in Luke 17:6:

> *It's not like you need a huge amount of faith. If you just had faith the size of a single, tiny mustard seed, you could **say** to this huge tree, "Pull up your roots and replant yourself in the sea," and it would fly through the sky and do what you said. So even a little faith can accomplish the seemingly impossible* (TV).

PENETRATING MOMENT: We spend a lot of time and energy working and not speaking. There is power in what you say. I believe the first place of attack the enemy targets is our mouths and our praise. If he can silence you, then he can sentence you. Sentence you? Yes, sentence you to a silent death in every area that you have not confessed victory over. It is what you say that moves the impossible.

Jesus teaches us that, if you only had faith in Him, even a little bit, your speaking could do a big bit. Today, I encourage you to open your mouth and start confessing.

Proverbs 18:20-21 teaches us that whatever is coming out of our mouths is what's filling up our lives. We can speak it to life or call it dead. The choice is ours. In whatever you say, fruit is being sown and produced. Whatever you speak, it will obey you. Watch what you are speaking because it's obeying.

PRAYER

Father, I pray now that we fill our lips with a praise that speaks of Your unfailing ability to do the impossible in our lives. We will open up our mouths and activate our faith to speak to the huge mountains in our lives and call them moved and gone. Just as you called Lazarus alive and told him to take off the grave clothes, we call the dead things to life, and everything that made them dead, we command to be removed, in Jesus' Name.

Break: *We interrupt the regularly scheduled program to bring you this breaking news story ... No rock will cry for me, I will open my mouth and shout for myself!!*

MY CUP RUNS OVER....

Those who sow in tears WILL reap with songs of joy
(Psalm 126:5).

The psalmist declares another mighty act of God. When God changes the seasons of our lives, we should change our posture and our song. I understand that seasons come and go, but when you are going through seasons where your emotional valve pops open and tears seem to be your moisturizer, you literally can't see the Son shining. Life does what life does and, when things happen that are out of your control, I want to encourage you to allow the Word of God to speak to you as you allow your cup to run over. Notice the order here: let Him speak AS your cup overflows!!

For the men who are reading this today, I have come to know that God has put emotions in me, so they must do what He placed them in me to do. Newsflash ~ Real men release tears in order to water for growth.

—◎—

PENETRATING MOMENT: God delights in being in the position to show forth His power and presence in those moments in our lives where all we can do is shed tears. He declares in His Word that, if I went out crying, I will come in shouting. I declare that my season of turnaround is pregnant with joy. So, cry if you must, but know that the tears are supplying water for the harvest.

Good Morning…

PRAYER

Father, as we go through painful times, let us take heart that our tears are our nutritious food. Please help us to know that weeping only endures for a night, but joy comes in the morning light. Today we resolve to let our tears flow as we sow for a harvest of joy.

Break: *We interrupt the regularly scheduled program to bring you this breaking news story … My tears are a temporary release before the Joy comes!!*

THE DARK PLACES

By your words I can see where I'm going; they throw a beam
of light on my dark path (Psalm 119:105, MSG).

I was driving along a dark lonely road one night and the only light was the high beam from the headlights of my car. It was then that I received a revelation that connected me to this text.

The Word of God will direct us according to our individual degree of maturity and our capacity compartment of faith. When the season seems dark, it is the Word that lays the bricks for the path that has already been marked out for us.

PENETRATING MOMENT: The steps of the righteous man are ordered by God and God Himself provides just enough light (the Word) on the path so that we can see the next step. IF He showed us the full view, we would probably get ahead of ourselves, Him and the plan.

So today, make sure that you allow the light that is in you from the One Who is in control of you to shine bright on high beam. Have a rhema Word in your mouth today because it is that Word that will light the way. The Lord is my light and my salvation.

Break: *We interrupt the regularly scheduled program to bring you this breaking news story ... I will TRUST in the light in dark places!!*

A CHOREOGRAPHED VICTORY

You're well-known as good and forgiving, bighearted to all who ask for help (Psalm 86:5, MSG).

When I think of the goodness of Jesus
And all He's done for me
My soul, my soul cries out
Hallelu, hallelujah
I thank God for saving me

-A song by Malcolm Speed

Whenever we choreograph a dance, we include elements that will make the dance speak and tell the audience the story. These are well-conceived moves and body postures we use to get "that" point across.

The choreographer listens to the rhythm, words, and message of the song and then devises complementary movements that speak the language or intention of the song. So, too, in a choreographed victory, the Believer has the victory dance because all the movements have been choreographed and orchestrated to lead up to VICTORY.

The victory includes: the mind (When I think), the actions (the goodness), the Person (Jesus), the collection (and all), the subject (that He) and the completed work (has done).

—◎—

PENETRATING MOMENT: Don't stop the Victory dance. Keep thinking, and your choreography will explode; keep reflecting, and your choreography will expand; keep rejoicing, and your choreography will light up the stage.

PRAYER

Father, thank You for inhabiting the place of my choreography. Today, I will command my hands to praise You, Lord. I will command my feet to move for You, Lord. I will command my mouth to shout to You, Lord. I will command my whole being to BLESS You, Lord.

Break: *We interrupt the regularly scheduled program to bring you this breaking news story ...This choreographer will keep the choreographed dance of Victory alive!!*

JUST STOP

Today I encourage you to ***STOP!***

You are inundated with your schedule, family, career, friends, ministry and much more. These "must have's" of life are building tension within you because of their nagging demands. You often see the signs that you must STOP, but oftentimes you ignore them because you must do life.

———◎———

PENETRATING MOMENT: Consider, if you will, what life would be like if you really could enjoy each moment of it. Imagine what the release of daily toxins would feel like if you dumped them daily. Well today, I encourage you to:

S ~ Seize the moment and not always grapple for the one you don't yet have. We live in moments in the present because that's what God gives us. Scriptures say tomorrow has enough compacted in it already, so live for the day's moment.

T ~ Trust IN the Lord's guidance every step of the way. I realize that planning is crucial but, if we are really perceptive in our planning, we will realize that our

Creator God has ALREADY ORDERED OUR STEPS. It is up to us to trust in the moments that we have and seize them for the revelation of the steps.

O ~ Obey whatever the Lord tells us. I have discovered that God speaks all day, every day, through everything. The challenge in our lives is that we must be positioned to obey what He speaks. STOP now and sit in your thoughts. Listen to what God is speaking right now.

P ~ Praise Him continually. What a powerful place to lock yourself into! A posture of praise throughout the day! What a blessing to serve a God who will take up residence in our lives if we would just GIVE Him the praise!

PRAYER

Father, thank You for the world so sweet, the food we eat, the birds that sing. Thank You God for EVERYTHING. We STOP now to seize the moment, to trust You, to obey Your command, and to praise Your Holy Name. Lead us to the rock that is higher than I, O Lord, in Jesus' Name. Amen

Break: *We interrupt the regularly scheduled program to bring you this breaking news story... STOP and Exhale.*

TRAFFIC IS NECESSARY

Today's penetrating word can be both literal and figurative. Literal because everyone hates traffic, and figurative because everyone hates the clutter in our lives that clogs, builds up, and backs up the normal flow of things. I want to share with you a revelation I had regarding traffic that shows why it is necessary.

PENETRATING MOMENT: I was in the thick of traffic on a Saturday afternoon. It was slow, crowded in every direction, a hindrance, and just annoying. I had run out of patience and decided to "cut a path" to get to my meeting as I was already an hour late. After many route changes and stalls up every path, I FINALLY got past the obstruction that had caused the traffic jam in the first place.

Upon re-entering the original scheduled route, I felt a sense of freedom, ease, and liberty to press the pedal and take any lane I desired. Inwardly, I rejoiced because I had passed the rough spot.

Traffic is necessary because it gives you the inner ability to press towards the goal. It gives you the fortitude to make adjustments and eventually to make it back on track. It gives you a method of trusting God even in crowded spaces. It gives you a reason to learn patience. It gives you the proper perspective on how to persevere, when the odds seem against you.

PRAYER

Father, in the name of Jesus today we thank You for the journey that You are allowing us to experience. We recognize and realize that traffic is necessary because it strengthens us, it enlarges us, it is preparing us to build stamina for the next phase of the journey. SO, thank You right now for where I am, in the place You have planned for me. I declare that endurance will be my portion, in Jesus' Name. Amen.

Break: *We interrupt the regularly scheduled program to bring you this breaking news story ... Traffic, we welcome you for our next phase!*

PAUSE

Pause ~ a temporary rest or break

PENETRATING MOMENT: In building a healthy lifestyle regimen, I ran across a concept that has helped me make it through the cravings and the moments of wanting to give in. It's called a "Pause."

The idea is that, whenever I felt the craving, I would "pause" and think about my goals and objectives, the new, fit me, the progress made, and the damage I would do if I gave in.

Today, I challenge you to push the "Pause" button so that you don't make a permanent decision based on a temporary situation. You are making progress and God is pleased with your yielding.

Just trust in the process and do as Paul admonished – press towards the mark – not regret the mark or mess up the mark.

Let yourself "Pause" and regroup for the greater good, and KEEP PRESSING.

PRAYER

Father, in Jesus' Name, we thank You for the ability that You have given us to push pause and get it all together. Today, we commit ourselves and our ways to taking advantage of pushing pause in every demanding situation. When the enemy tries to come in like a flood, we will pause and declare Your word. We will speak life, not death. We thank you that You are a very present help in time of trouble and now, in Jesus' name, we speak peace within the pause.

Break: *We interrupt the regularly scheduled program to bring you this breaking news story... I will not abort the mission, but will push pause and persevere until ...*

IT'S BEEN CLEARED FOR YOU

Today, I want to empower you to know that, when God speaks, He will sometimes use earthly encounters to show you what He intends to manifest in your life (if you only believe!).

―⊙―

PENETRATING MOMENT: Thought #28 speaks about traffic and its necessity. Well, for about three months, as I would approach the expressway going in to work, the traffic would really be tight and getting on the entrance ramp to join the crowd was a nightmare. Most mornings, as I approached the expressway, all I could see were brake lights for miles.

I would spend most of my morning drives in conversation with God: about the day, my life and His Master plan for me, and just listening to His awesome responses. On many occasions as I would pray going in, the lanes would be clear and I would be able to cross four lanes of traffic without anyone hindering me, blocking me, blowing their horns and getting upset using their body language.

I would **see** the clear path as I entered and would **ease** my way to the furthest lane and proceed. Every time I experienced this, God would speak to me and say these exact words: "I have cleared the way and given you access to your next lane change. It's time to get in your place and move FORWARD." I thought, "WOW God, You have a way of speaking loud and clear!"

Today, be like Peter as in Thought #14 (Matthew 14) where the way has already been made. Take advantage of the new season, and watch how God provides EXACTLY what YOU need as you slide into new territory. Trust God as He directs and fills your life with the right people of influence, power and resources to help you achieve what you saw in your vision. Listen to His voice and Obey.

PRAYER

Father, today I pray that the person who has gotten to this day in the journey recognizes and embraces the shifts that are taking place in their lives right now. I pray that, as we partner with You, we will allow Your mighty hand to move in a supernatural way in our lives every day, in Jesus' Name. Amen

Break: *We interrupt the regularly scheduled program to bring you this breaking news story... I will listen, obey and execute!!*

NET-BREAKING SEASON

As a prophetic voice in the Kingdom of God, I want to use this last day of *Penetrating Thoughts, Volume 1* to speak a word into your life. One that I feel is applicable in every season that you may find yourself in your journey.

Luke 5 speaks of when the disciples partnered with God they witnessed a "net-breaking" experience. They obeyed God and the supernatural happened.

1 Kings 17:16 tells the story of a woman who partnered with God through the man of God and she witnessed the jar of flour that was not used up and the jugs of oil that did not run out.

I declare and I decree that, as you partner with God, you will experience the supernatural overflow of a net-breaking season where you will become a conduit which God uses to bless others.

I sense that, as you obey God, you will encounter opportunities to always live in a realm of the more abundant; a realm where FAVOR is your constant; a realm where everything you touch will prosper and everywhere your feet tread you will possess; a realm where, when you speak, it manifests suddenly; a realm where your FAITH is activated and FEAR cannot topple you; a realm where abundant provision is your daily portion.

Go forth and let the Word of the Lord penetrate your mind until your heart receives!!

Much love,
Michael

EPILOGUE

What a journey this has been! Continue to be intentional about freeing yourself from the daily thoughts that obstruct your thinking and allow the penetration of the Word of God, the penetration of positive affirmations, and the penetration of life-altering, power-filled words to fill your life. As you free your thoughts, you will move in a new strength and ability.

BIOGRAPHY

Bishop Michael A. Strickland is the proud son of the late Reverend Dr. Hopie Strickland, Jr. and Mrs. Linda D. Strickland. He is married to the former Brenda E. Clark and they are the parents of Briana Michelle, Morgan Lynn and Audria Hope Celeste. Affectionately called "Pastor Mike" or "Bishop" by the members of the Victory Tabernacle Church International, he serves faithfully and diligently in leading this congregation to become the church that God is pleased with and smiles upon. The vision that God has given him for the ministry is to "Expose God; Explore God's Word and Exemplify God's Character in the Earth."

Bishop Strickland received his undergraduate degree in Music Education from Valdosta State University in Valdosta, Georgia, a Master's Degree in Library Science from Jacksonville State University in Jacksonville, Alabama, and a Master's Degree in Biblical Studies from Beulah Heights University, Atlanta, Georgia.

Bishop Strickland accepted his call to proclaim the Gospel of Jesus Christ in December 1995 and preached his initial sermon on the 4th Sunday in January 1996. In 2000, he was called as Pastor of the Little Bethel Baptist Church in Mableton, Georgia and served there until 2004. After being led by the Lord to resign as pastor, Bishop Strickland was the "Joshua" who was assigned to serve as his father's assistant at Victory until his father's transition on July 12, 2007. On September 9, 2007, he became the pastor of the Victory Tabernacle Church.

He was elevated to the office of Bishop on July 12, 2009 by Bishop Ruth W. Smith, Presiding Prelate of the Light of the World International Interdenominational Association. He is proud of the fact that God has His hands in the plans for his life and submits himself completely to God's authority. He has done international ministry, preaching and ministering in London, England, as well as, Andobakedash and Chennai, India.

As a bi-vocational pastor, Bishop Strickland has been employed as a Music Specialist with the Atlanta Public Schools for more than 25 years. Two of his greatest honors are being twice named the "Teacher of the Year" and being highlighted in the Collegiate Edition of Outstanding Educators. As a gifted encourager, Bishop is known as the E3 guy: He will Empower, Encourage and Equip you to be the best you that you can be.

Bishop Strickland continues to grow in Christ, he enjoys worship, serving, preaching, singing, and empowering the people of God. All glory, honor, and praise belong to God as he continues to do what he loves doing and that is being who God would have him be.

For speaking engagements or book signings, contact Bishop Strickland at:

bookings@mastrickland.org
www.mastrickland.org

www.ingramcontent.com/pod-product-compliance
Lightning Source LLC
LaVergne TN
LVHW061228060426
835509LV00012B/1465